TRIVIA

GOES BANANAS

711 Brain Bafflers

That'll Stump Ya!

TRIVIA
GOES BANANAS

711 Brain Bafflers

That'll Stump Ya!

APPLESAUCE PRESS

LOU HARRY

13-Digit ISBN: 978-1-60433-342-8
10-Digit ISBN: 1-60433-342-1

This book may be ordered by mail from the publisher. Please include $4.95 for postage and handling. Please support your local bookseller first!

Books published by Cider Mill Press Book Publishers are available at special discounts for bulk purchases in the United States by corporations, institutions, and other organizations. For more information, please contact the publisher.

Applesauce Press is an imprint of
Cider Mill Press Book Publishers
"Where good books are ready for press"
12 Port Farm Road
Kennebunkport, Maine 04046

Visit us on the Web!
www.cidermillpress.com

Design by Tilly Grassa, TGCreative Services
Illustrations courtesy of Anthony Owsley
Cover design by Whitney Cookman

Printed in China

1 2 3 4 5 6 7 8 9 0
First Edition

CONTENTS

1. Big Screen/Little Screen 6

2. Sports 16

3. Food For Thought................. 30

4. Game Time 44

5. Animals 58

6. Comics 72

7. Celebrities 88

8. Music 100

9. It Happened In 116

Answers........................... 148

CHAPTER

1

Big Screen/Little Screen

THREE FILMS ARE TIED FOR THE RECORDS FOR MOST ACADEMY AWARDS, WITH 11. NAME THE FILM THAT...

1) Had a big scene involving a chariot race.

2) Climaxed with the sinking of an ocean liner.

3) Was the third film in a series.

****

4) JOHN WILLIAMS HAS THE MOST OSCAR NOMINATIONS OF ANY LIVING PERSON. WHAT IS HIS JOB?

A) COMPOSING   B) DIRECTING

C) ACTING   D) COSTUME DESIGN

****

5) According to *The Hollywood Reporter* in 2011, what is the most pirated movie of all time?

****

6) True or false: There's a movie called *Yikkity Yikes.*

7) True or false: There's a movie called *Eegah*.

****

8> True or false: There's a movie called *Attack of the Killer Tomatoes*.

COMPLETE THE TITLES OF THESE FILMS, WHICH ARE ALL PART OF THE NATIONAL FILM REGISTRY.

9) *Sweet Smell of* _____

10) *One Flew Over the* _____ *Nest*

11) *Blade* _____

12) *An American in* _____

13) *Meet Me in St.* _____

14) *Invasion of the Body* _____

15) *The African* _____

16) *To Kill a* _____

17) *North by* _____

18) *The Last of the* _____

19) True or False: There's a movie called *Jesse James Meets Frankenstein's Daughter.*

20) True or false: **There's a movie called *Killer Klowns from Outer Space.***

COMPLETE THE TITLES OF THESE WILL SMITH MOVIES.

21) *Bad* _____

22) _____ *Day*

23) *Wild Wild* _____

24) *Enemy of the* _____

25) *Men in* _____

26) *Shark* _____

27) *The* _____ *of Happyness*

28) *I Am* _____

29) *Seven* _____

30) What is Bob the Builder's three-word answer to "Can we build it?"

31) How old is Caillou supposed to be?
    a) 2   b) 3   c) 4   d) 10

32) What is Arthur the Aardvark's last name?

33) WHO HAD A TV SERIES FIRST, DORA OR DIEGO?

34) Which of the following did not host the Nickelodeon Kids' Choice Awards
a) Jack Black   b) Tom Cruise
c) Justin Timberlake   d) Ben Stiller

35) True or false: Snoop dog was slimed at the 2011 Nickelodeon Kids' Choice Awards

I REALLY NEED TO FIRE MY AGENT!

36) What are the evil robots called on *Mighty Morphin' Power Rangers* called?
    a) Zods b) Zords
    c) Zens d) Zingas

37> Which of the following was not a Degrassi series or special?

a> *The Kids of Degrassi Street*

b> *Degrassi: The Next Generation*

c> *Degrassi Takes Manhattan*

d> *Degrassi: Always Greener*

38) Were there more episodes made of *Sabrina the Teenage Witch* or *Touched by an Angel*?

39) Were there more episodes made of *Everybody Loves Raymond* or *Everybody Hates Chris*?

40) True or false: There was once a TV show called *When Things Were Rotten.*

41) True or false: There was once a TV show called *The Secret Diary of Desmond Pfeffer.*

42) True or false: There was once a TV show called *Today is Tomorrow's Yesterday*.

* *

43) True or false: **There was once a TV show called *The Show Show Show*.**

* *

44) What does TLC stand for?

* *

45) WHAT DOES BET STAND FOR?

* *

46) True or false: There is a Live Monkey Cam Channel.

* * * * * * * *

47) What does HLN stand for?

* *

48) True or false: There is a Pentagon Channel

49> Which of the following is not an ESPN channel?

   a> ESPN Plus   b> ESPN2

   c> ESPN-W   d> ESPN Classic

★ ★ ★ ★ ★ ★ ★ ★ ★ ★ ★ ★ ★ ★ ★ ★ ★ ★ ★ ★

50) What does HSN stand for?

★ ★ ★ ★ ★ ★ ★ ★ ★ ★ ★ ★ ★ ★ ★ ★ ★ ★ ★ ★

51) What does QVC stand for?

★ ★ ★ ★ ★ ★ ★ ★ ★ ★ ★ ★ ★ ★ ★ ★ ★ ★ ★ ★

52) True or false: **ARTN is the Armenian-Russian Television Network.**

★ ★ ★ ★ ★ ★ ★ ★ ★ ★ ★ ★ ★ ★ ★ ★ ★ ★ ★ ★

53) True or false: There used to be a Lottery Channel.

★ ★ ★ ★ ★ ★ ★ ★ ★ ★ ★ ★ ★ ★ ★ ★ ★ ★ ★ ★

54) True or false: There was once a TV show called *Shasty McNasty*.

★ ★ ★ ★ ★ ★ ★ ★ ★ ★ ★ ★ ★ ★ ★ ★ ★ ★ ★ ★

55) True or false: **There was once a TV show called *Albert Einstein, Boy Genius*.**

★ ★ ★ ★ ★ ★ ★ ★ ★ ★ ★ ★ ★ ★ ★ ★ ★ ★ ★ ★

56) True or false: There was once a TV show called *It's Like, You Know*.

CHAPTER

2

★ ★ ★ ★ ★ ★ ★ ★

Sports

57) TRUE OR FALSE: THE LOS ANGELES DODGERS WERE ONCE KNOWN AS THE ROBINS.

• •

58) True or false: The Philadelphia Phillies were once known as the Blue Jays.

• •

59) What Cleveland Indians star holds the career record for doubles?
 a) Albert Belle   b) Lou Boudreau
 c) Kenny Lofton   d) Tris Speaker

• •

60) What baseball team was once known as the Colts?
a) Baltimore Orioles b) Boston Red Sox
c) Chicago Cubs   d) New York Yankees

• •

61> What baseball team was once known as the Colt .45s?
a> Arizona Diamondbacks b> Houston Astros
c> Kansas City Royals   d> Texas Rangers

62) What team was the first to win the World Series after finishing last the previous season?
a) 1914 Braves   b) 1969 Mets
c) 1991 Twins   d) 1997 Marlins

63) What player, the career leader in triples, was nicknamed for his hometown?

a) Cap Anson
b) Wahoo Sam Crawford
c) Pea Ridge Day
d) Vinegar Bend Mizell

• •

64) The left field wall in what ballpark is known as "The Green Monster"?

a) Coors Field
b) Dodger Stadium
c) Fenway Park
d) Yankee Stadium

• • • • • • • • • •

65) The New York Yankees have won more World Championships than any other team. What team ranks second?

a) Cardinals
b) Dodgers
c) Giants
d) Red Sox

• •

66) What disability was shared by Browns outfielder Pete Gray and Angels pitcher Jim Abbott?

a) Blindness
b) Deafness
c) Muteness
d) One arm

67) A farming accident as a youth gave Hall of Fame pitcher Mordecai Brown what nickname?

a) Gimpy b) Lefty

c) Stumpy d) Three Finger

68) In 1997, Jackie Robinson's #42 was retired by every MLB team except the Yankees, who were allowed to let what player to continue wearing it?

a) Derek Jeter b) Mariano Rivera

c) Alex Rodriguez d) Bernie Williams

MATCH THE NICKNAME TO THE PLAYER.

69) THE BIRD A) HARRY BRECHEEN

70) THE CAT B) MARK FIDRYCH

71) THE HAT C) BILL SKOWRON

72) MOOSE D) HARRY WALKER

73) True or false: Joe Torre, who reached 14 straight postseasons as a manager, never played a postseason game as a player.

74) **Which of these men did not manage both the Yankees and Mets?**
a) **Yogi Berra**   b) **Joe Girardi**
c) **Dallas Green**   d) **Joe Torre**

75) Who was the first manager to win the World Series with teams from both leagues?

76> True or false: the 1972 World Series between the A's and Reds and the 1984 World Series between the Tigers and Padres featured the same two managers.

77) Who was the first African-American manager to win the World Series?

78) What team won the first two Super Bowls?
a) Chicago Bears   b) Dallas Cowboys
c) Green Bay Packers d) Pittsburgh Steelers

79) What is the only team in the Super Bowl era to go undefeated?

a) Baltimore Colts   b) Indianapolis Colts
c) Miami Dolphins   d) New England Patriots

* *

80) What team was the first to go 0-16 in a season?

a) Detroit Lions   b) Indianapolis Colts
c) Kansas City Chiefs   d) Tampa Bay Buccaneers

Match the team to its stadium.

81) Arrowhead Stadium   a. Kansas City Chiefs
82) Candlestick Park   b. San Francisco 49ers
83) FedEx Field   c. Tennessee Titans
84) LP Field   d. Washington Redskins

85) What was Brett Favre's first NFL team?

   a) Atlanta Falcons
   b) Green Bay Packers
   c) Minnesota Vikings
   d) New York Giants

86) What Chicago Bears great was nicknamed "Sweetness"?
a) Dick Butkus
b) Walter Payton
c) Brian Piccolo
d) Gale Sayers

Match the coach with his team.

87) Bill Cowher	a. Chicago Bears
88) George Halas	b. Dallas Cowboys
89) Tom Landry	c. Oakland Raiders
90) John Madden	d. Pittsburgh Steelers

91) IN CANADIAN FOOTBALL, A TEAM CAN SCORE ONE POINT BY KICKING THE BALL UNTOUCHED INTO THE OTHER TEAM'S END ZONE. WHAT IS THIS PLAY CALLED?
A) BLANC   B) BLEU   C) ROUGE   D) VERDE

92) What division is the Milwaukee Bucks in?

93) What division is the Golden State Warriors in?

94) What division is the Portland Trail Blazers in?

95 > What division is the Dallas Mavericks in?

96) What division is the Miami Heat in?

97) Did the American Basketball Association last more or less than a decade?

98) What colors were the ABA basketball?

99) What is it called when a player dribbles, holds the ball, and then dribbles again?

100) The National Basketball Association was formed by a merger of the National Basketball League and...
  a) The Basketball League of Teams
  b) The Basketball Association of America
  c) The American Basketball Association
  d) The North American Gamesmen's League

101) What is the diameter of a basketball rim?

    a) 14 inches   b) 16 inches
    c) 18 inches   d) 20 inches

102) True or false: The backboard was added to the game to prevent interference from spectators.

103) WHO HAD MORE NBA FIELD GOALS IN A SINGLE SEASON, KAREEM ABDUL-JABBAR OR WILT CHAMBERLAIN?

104) Who had more NBA field goals in a single season, Michael Jordan or Bob McAdoo?

105) Who had more NBA field goals in a single season, Elgin Baylor or George Gervin?

106) Who had more free throws in a single NBA season, Jerry West or Wilt Chamberlain?

107> Who had more free throws in a single NBA season, Michael Jordan or Oscar Robertson?

108) Who had more free throws in a single NBA season, Moses Malone or Charles Barkley?

• •

109) Who had more offensive rebounds in a single NBA season, Moses Malone or Charles Barkley?

• • • • • • • • • • • • • • • • • • • •

110) What school has won the most NCAA championships?

• • • • • • • • • • • • • • • • • •

111) In soccer, which has won more World Cup championships, Brazil or Germany?

112) True or false: Germany has finished in the World Cup in the top two more often than Italy.

113) Has Sweden ever been in the World Cup top two?

114) Has Hungary ever been in the World Cup top two?

115) WHICH HAS BEEN IN THE WORLD CUP TOP THREE MORE OFTEN, GERMANY OR BRAZIL?

• • • • • • • • • • • • • • • • • • •

116) True or false: Pelé's real name is Edson.

• • • • • • • • • • • • • • ➤

117) In Brazil, Pelé was known as:
 a) The King
 b) The Duke
 c) The Bishop
 d) The Prince

• • • • • • • • • • • • • • • • • • • •

118) In what year did Pelé retire from soccer?
a) 1977 b) 1982 c) 1986 d) 1990

119> Who did the U.S. team defeat in 1980 to win the Olympic Gold medal in hockey?

★ ★

120) Is the NHL Hall of Fame in the U.S. or Canada?

★ ★

121) True or false: There is a regulation size ice rink in the Hockey Hall of Fame.

★ ★

122) Who was not a 2011 inductee in the Hockey Hall of Fame?
   a) Mark Howe
   b) Myles Strong
   c) Joe Nieuwendyk
   d) Ed Belfour

123) True or false: Gordie Howe played over 1,700 games.

124) Who played more games, Wayne Gretzky or Dave Andreychuk?

★ ★

125) How many inches tall is a bowling pin?

126) How much does a bowling pin weigh?
            a) 1–2 lbs
            b) 2–3 lbs
            c) 3–4 lbs
            d) 4–5 lbs

★ ★ ★ ★ ★ ★ ★ ★ ★ ★ ★ ★ ★ ★ ★ ★ ★ ★ ★ ★

127) IN A BOWLING PIN RACK, WHICH PIN IS NUMBER 7?
            A) THE REAR RIGHT
            B) THE REAR LEFT
            C) THE CENTER
            D) THE SECOND PIN IN THE THIRD ROW

128) True or false: If a bowling ball bounces out of the gutter and knocks over a pin, the pin counts for the bowler.

CHAPTER

3

Food for Thought

129) True or false: Fiber is the part of plant foods that our bodies digest.

* *

130) True or false: **A Mayan legend has it that humans are made from corn.**

* *

131) Which of the following is not a kind of orange:
a) Valencia   b) Blood
c) Cara Cara d) Alphonso

132 > Which has more calories, fresh coconut or fresh figs?

133) Which has more calories, blueberries or dates?

* *

134) True or False: There is a Mexican cheese known as Chihuahua.

* *

135) What does *salsa* mean?

136) True or false: The word *enchilada* means "in tortillas."

137) True or false: The Aztecs ate tamales.

138) Is flan a native Mexican dessert?

* *

139) Are traditional Chinese dishes served as courses or all together at once?

* *

140) WHAT DOES "CON CARNE," AS IN CHILI CON CARNE, MEAN?

* * * * * * * * * * * *

141) Cap'n Crunch was launched in...
    a) 1963
    b) 1968
    c) 1972
    d) 1979

* * * * * * * * * * * *

142) True or false: The original breakfast cereal—called Granola—was sold in blocks and needed to be chipped away by consumers and soaked in milk.

* *

143) True or false: Fruit Brute was originally one of the monster cereals.

144 > What cereal has Tony the Tiger as a mascot?

* *

145) Is muesli made from cooked or uncooked rolled oats?

* *

146) Wheaties advertises itself as "The Breakfast of _____."

* *

147) What cereal was advertised with the line "Kid tested, mother approved."

* *

148) Which of the following was not a Cheerio's variation:
- a) Chocolate Cheerios
- b) Yogurt Burst Cheerios
- c) Cheerio Max
- d) Banana Nut Cheerios

* *

149) What is the Cocoa Puffs' bird's name?
- a) Kooky
- b) Sonny
- c) Socko
- d) Wacko

150) True or false: Corn Pops were originally called Sweetie Pops.

• •

151) TRUE OR FALSE: CORN POPS IS DIFFERENT IN THE U.S. THAN IT IS IN CANADA.

* *

152) True or false: Grape-Nuts contains neither grapes nor nuts.

153) Match the mascot to the cereal.

1) Dig 'em
2) Sam
3) Snap, Crackle and Pop
4) Sugar Bear
5) Tony the Tiger

a) Froot Loops
b) Rice Krispies
c) Sugar Frosted Flakes
d) Sugar Smacks
e) Super Sugar Crisp

154) How hot is the hottest pepper in the world?
   a) 1,700 Scoville heat units
   b) 17,000 Scoville heat units
   c) 146,300 Scoville heat units
   d) 1,463,700 Scoville heat units

155> How many seeds in an apricot?

156) True or false: on a food label, high fiber means 20 grams or more per serving.

157) Does avocado ripen on the tree or off the tree?

158) What was the name of the little boy used as a guinea pig to try Life cereal?

159) What cereal is "not for silly rabbits"?

160) What cereal gets its name from the fact it has 100% of the recommended daily allowances of most necessary nutrients?

161) What is Cap'n Crunch's first name?

162) Who is the mayor of McDonaldland?

163) WHAT CHICKEN RESTAURANT CHAIN IS FAMOUSLY CLOSED ON SUNDAYS?
- A) CHICK-FIL-A
- B) CHURCH'S
- C) KFC
- D) POPEYES

164) What was the Taco Bell dog's catchphrase?

165) What drive-in burger chain's signature items include limeade, tater tots, and foot-long chili dogs?

166) Who founded McDonald's?
- a) Ray Buktenica
- b) Ray Kroc
- c) Ray Romano
- d) Ray Stevens

167 > True or false: Slurpees can only be sold at 7-Eleven.

168) What cowboy star lent his name to a chain of roast beef restaurants?

169) The formula for what burger is "Two all-beef patties, special sauce, lettuce, cheese, pickles, onions on a sesame seed bun"?

170) What shape are White Castle hamburgers?

171) The owner of McDonald's also owned what Major League baseball team?

a) Milwaukee Brewers
b) San Diego Padres
c) San Francisco Giants
d) Texas Rangers

172) Dave Thomas named Wendy's after his eight-year-old daughter, who was nicknamed Wendy. What was her real name?
a) Betty Lou b) Melinda Lou
c) Annie Lou d) Wanda Lou

173) What kind of animal is seen in most Chick-fil-A advertising?

THAT'S THE ONE! THE SECOND FROM THE RIGHT!

174) True or false:
The first TGI Friday's was in New York.

175) TRUE OR FALSE: ALL TGI FRIDAY'S LOCATIONS FEATURE REAL TIFFANY LAMPS.

176) True or false:
Red Lobster's Crab Linguini Alfredo has more calories than four quarter-pound steamed lobsters.

177) True or false:
Red Lobster calls its lower-fat choices LightHouse Selections.

178) True or false: There are Red Lobster restaurants in Japan.

179> Which of the following is not an Outback side dish?

a> Garlic Mashed Potatoes

b> Grilled Asparagus

c> Walkabout Lima Beans

d> Sweet Potato Fries

★ ★

180) True or false: You can buy a rocking chair at Cracker Barrel?

★ ★ ★ ★ ★ ★ ★ ★ ★ ★ ★ ★ ★

181) True or false: There's over 1,800 calories in an Outback Steakhouse Bloomin' Onion.

★ ★ ★ ★ ★ ★ ★ ★ ★ ★ ★ ★

182) Bubba Gump Shrimp Company was inspired by a reference in what Oscar-winning film?

183) True or false: Most of the Bubba Gump Shrimp Company locations are in Malaysia.

184) Is there a Planet Hollywood in Hollywood?

★ ★

185) Was mustard first considered a food or a medicine?

★ ★

186) Does ketchup get darker or lighter when it's exposed to sun?

★ ★ ★ ★ ★ ★ ★ ★ ★

187) DIJON IS A REGION OF WHAT COUNTRY?

★ ★

188) Which is hotter, white mustard seed or brown mustard seeds?

★ ★

189) True or false: **Pope John XXII named his nephew as *moutardier du pape* or mustard-maker to the pope.**

190 > True or false: Chewing gum makes an appearance in Mark Twain's *The Adventures of Tom Sawyer?*

191) Wrigley's Juicy Fruit gum first appeared in...
- a) 1872
- b) 1893
- c) 1912
- d) 1932

192) True or false: In 1915, Wrigley sent gum to everyone listed in U.S. phone books.

193) What is the most popular cookie in the world?

194) Before undergoing a name change, what were milk chocolate M&M's called?

195) Which is not a variety of M&Ms?

    a) Almond

    b) Coconut

    c) Crisped rice

    d) Hazelnut

196) What company makes Oreos?

    a) General Mills

    b) Hershey

    c) Keebler

    d) Nabisco

197) What ancestor of bowling is the name of a candy?

    a) Kit Kat

    b) Skittles

    c) Starburst

    d) Twix

Match the slogan to the breath freshener.

198) Brush your breath	a) Altoids
199) The curiously strong mints	b) Certs
200) The 1 ½ Calorie Breath Mint	c) Dentyne
201) Two-two-two mints in one	d) Tic Tac

CHAPTER

4

Game Time

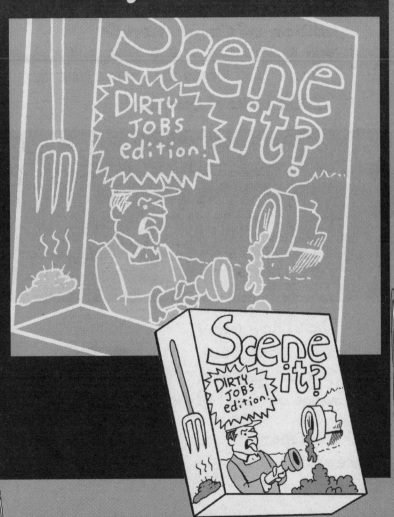

202) How many spaces are there on the Candy Land board?

a) 72   b) 91   c) 112   d) 134

* *

203) What was the Molasses Swamp changed to in the 2002 edition of Candy Land?

* * * * * * * * * * * * * * * * * * *

204 > True or false: Plumpy was removed from the 2002 edition of Candy Land.

205) Which of the following was not a Candy Land spin-off:

a) Candy Land: Winnie-the-Pooh edition
b) Candy Land: VCR Board Game
c) Candy Land: Eat-n-Play Edition
d) Candy Land Castle Game

206) How many pawns does each player get in a game of Sorry!

* * * * * * * * * * *

207) How many spaces wide is a Stratego board?

208) How many flags does each Stratego player have?

209) In Stratego, what is higher ranked, a Colonel or a Major?
****

210) In Stratego, what is higher ranked, a Miner or a Lieutenant?

211) How many points do you get for a large straight in Yahtzee?

212) HOW MANY POINTS DO YOU NEED TO SCORE IN THE UPPER SECTION OF YAHTZEE IN ORDER TO GET A BONUS?
****

213) What happens if you role a six in Chutes and Ladders?
****

214) How many pieces are there in a total Cootie?

215) True or false: The creator of Cootie originally designed the bug as a fishing lure.

216 > How many buckets in a game of Hi Ho Cherry O?

217) What is the highest hand in poker (with no wild cards)?

218) What beats paper in Rock Paper Scissors?

219) How many people can play Rock'em Sock'em Robots at one time?

220) In Rock'em Sock'em Robots, one robot is blue. What color is the other?

221) How many buttons are on each side of Rock'em Sock'em Robots?

222) What color is the boxing platform in Rock'em Sock'em Robots?

223) Which of the following is not a LEGO game:
a) Heroica   b) Pirate Plank
c) Terror Ship   d) Ramses Return

224) HOW MANY WHITE CHECKERS START OUT A GAME OF BACKGAMMON IN WHITE'S HOME BOARD?

225) How many white checkers start out a game of backgammon in red's home board?

226) True or false:
In backgammon, if you can only play one number, you have to use the highest usable dice role.

227) True or false: In backgammon, you can only have five checkers on a point.

228> True or false: There is a Bible edition of Apples to Apples

229) True or false: There is a Disney edition of Apples to Apples.

230) True or false: Sour Apples to Apples contains apple dice.

231) Which is not an edition of Scene It:

a) James Bond edition

b) Turner Classic Movies edition

c) Sitcom edition

d) Pirates of the Caribbean edition

232) What Oscar-winner starred in the movie *Dungeons and Dragons?*

a) Daniel Day-Lewis   b) Anthony Hopkins

c) Jeremy Irons   d) Ben Kingsley

233) How many possible character alignments are there in D&D?

234) What alignment is the polar opposite of "Lawful-Good" in D&D?

235) WHAT CHARACTER CLASS IS ALWAYS TRUE NEUTRAL?
A) BARD B) CAVALIER
C) CLERIC D) MONK

236) Which spell is easier to learn, magic missiles or fireballs?

237) What character class is most useful against undead monsters?
a) Cavalier   b) Cleric
c) Fighter   d) Paladin

238) True or false: the magazine for D&D enthusiasts is called *The Dungeon.*

239 > What is the rule change in Duplicate Scrabble?

a > Players each get 14 letters

b > All players play with the same letters

c > Two boards are connected at a corner

d > There are twice as many letters in the game

240) Is it possible to play Scrabble with Chinese letters?

* *

241) True or False: In French Scrabble, the X and the Y are each worth 10 points.

• •

242) How many spaces wide is a Scrabble board?

* *

243) Is Scrabble an acceptable Scrabble word?

* * * * * * * * * * *

244) How many Zs are there in a Scrabble game?

245) How many tiles are there in a Scrabble set?
a) 100   b) 104   c) 130   d) 150

246) True or false: the World Scrabble Championship is played in Washington every year.

* *

247) TRUE OR FALSE: NATIONAL SCRABBLE CHAMPIONSHIP OFFICIALS ONCE DISALLOWED A WORD BECAUSE IT WAS CONSIDERED OFFENSIVE, EVEN THOUGH IT WAS IN THE DICTIONARY.

* *

248) Is Venezuela a territory in Risk?

249) Is Quebec a territory?

250) Is Italy a territory?

* *

251> Can Iceland attack Ukraine?

252) True or false: An early version of the Game of Life was called the Checkered Game of Life?

253) When was the contemporary version of the Game of Life first released?
a) 1950
b) 1960
c) 1970
d) 1980

254) How many numbers on the Game of Life spinner?

255) True or false: The $500 bills have been dropped from the Game of Life?

256) Which of the following was not a Clue variation?
a) Clue: Seinfeld Collectors Edition
b) Clue: The Office Edition
c) Clue: Futurama Edition
d) Clue: Harry Potter Edition

257) True or false: In Clue: Dungeons and Dragons, Mr. Green has been replaced by a lump of gelatinous ooze.

258) True of false: According to the rules of Monopoly, you collect money from the center of the board when you land on Free Parking.

259) WHAT ARE THE FIRST TWO PURCHASABLE PROPERTIES ON THE MONOPOLY BOARD?

● ●

260) Name the four Monopoly railroads.

261) In Monopoly, is "You've won second prize in a beauty contest" a Chance card or a Community Chest card?

★ ★

262) True or false: There's a version of Monopoly with a round board.

★ ★

263 > How many spaces on a Monopoly board?

★ ★

264) How many properties in a Monopoly game?

★ ★

265) True or false: The cost of the luxury tax has changed in Monopoly.

★ ★ ★ ★ ★ ★ ★ ★ ★

266) True or false: Word Search puzzles were first published in the 1860s.

267) How many small squares are there in a standard Sudoku puzzles?

268) What is the highest number in a standard Sudoku puzzle?

269) How many numbers are used in Mini Sudoku?

★ ★

270) True or false: When a Sudoku puzzle first appeared in the British newspaper *The Times,* it was called Su Doku.

CHAPTER

5

Animals

271) True or false: Giraffes don't have eyelashes.

272 > How many pointed teeth does an adult hedgehog have?

a> 0   b> 12   c> 24   d> 36

273) Does a hedgehog have cheekbones?

274) True or false: A hedgehog's spine is hollow.

275) True or false: A pygmy hippo can weigh as much as 600 lbs.

276) How many toes does a hippo have?

277) True or false: A hippo can't wag its tail.

278) True or false: A hippo can gallop up to 30 mph.

279) True or false: **A hyena has retractable claws.**

280) TRUE OR FALSE: A HYENA'S STOMACH CAN DIGEST BONES.

281) Are male or female hyenas heavier?

282) An aardwolf feeds mostly on...
a) **Rabbits**
b) **Termites**
c) **Hyenas**
d) **Lizards**

283) Which has longer horns, a male or female ibex?

284> Are male wild goat horns smooth or ridged?

285) Are jaguar claws retractable?

286) True or False: The canine teeth of a jaguar are used primarily for eating.

287) In bright light, do a jaguar's pupils shrink to a dot or to a slit?

288) Proportionately, which has longer front legs, a cheetah or a jaguar?

289) Which is bigger, an adult male kangaroo or adult female kangaroo.

290) How many digits are on a kangaroo's hand?

291) True or false: **A red kangaroo can reach 40 mph.**

- - -

292) DO FEMALE OPOSSUMS HAVE POUCHES?

- - -

293) How many toes does an opossum have on each foot?

- - -

294) Opossums have the most teeth of any marsupial. How many does each have?
- a) 44
- b) 50
- c) 62
- d) 84

- - -

295) The lion is the second largest cat. What's the first?

296) A lion's skull can weigh up to...
- a) 2 lbs
- b) 4 lbs
- c) 6 lbs
- d) 12 lbs

297) What is usually longer, a meerkat's body or its tail?

****

298) Meerkats are different from other mongooses because...

  a) They only have four toes on each foot

  b) They have opposable thumbs

  c) They are primarily found in Asia

  d) They do not dig

  ****

299) True or false: Most mongoose species are herbivores.

****

300) True or false: All zebras have the same stripe pattern.

****

301) True or false: A pronghorn signals danger by raising its white rump hairs.

302) Which of the following is not a common fur color for a puma?
- a) Red-brown
- b) Blue-grey
- c) Yellow
- d) Black

303) Which is usually longer, a ring-tailed coati or a kinkajou?

* *

304) IS THE TIP OF A RACCOON'S STRIPED TAIL ALWAYS DARK OR ALWAYS LIGHT?

* *

305) True or false: The antelope is the largest living deer.

306) How long does it take for a red deer to get twelve points on its antlers?
- a) 2 years
- b) 4 years
- c) 6 years
- d) 8 years

307) True or false: Red deer are born with white spots that fade away.

308 > True or false: The red fox has a scent gland on its tail.

309) Which is larger, the Sumatran rhino or the Indian rhino?

310) Which has more horns, the Sumatran rhino or the Indian rhino?

311) Which has a longer horn, the Sumatran rhino or the white rhino?

312) True or false:
Rhino ears can only be moved together.

313) How many hooves on a rhino's foot?

314) True or false: Shrews eat food adding up to 80-90% of their body weight every week.

315) Is a Tasmanian devil a mammal, a marsupial, or a rodent?

316) TRUE OR FALSE: THE TASMANIAN DEVIL HAS NO WHISKERS.

317) True or false: The Tasmanian devil's tail can only move side to side.

318) On what continent are Tasmanian devils found?

319) A Tasmanian devil's jaw can open:
a) 20-30 degrees
b) 30-50 degrees
c) 50-70 degrees
d) 75-80 degrees

320 > True or false: Tasmanian devils will sometimes take over the former nests of wombats.

321) True or false: Tigers can easily walk on hot surfaces.

OW! OW! HOT SAND!

322) True or false: The smallest tiger species is the Sumatran tiger.

323) How many claws does a tiger have on each forepaw?

324) True or false: Small cats can't roar because of its hyoid bone.

325) True or false: Tiger teeth can be up to 10 inches long.

326) Which is larger, a gray wolf or a red wolf?

327) Does a wolf have more teeth on its upper jaw or its lower jaw?

328) WHICH TENDS TO HAVE THE LONGEST EARS, A WOMBAT, A BANDICOOT, OR A BILBY?

329) A cow can't produce milk until it...
a) Has a calf
b) Is over 390 lbs.
c) Both of the above
d) None of the above

330) When hand-milked, about how many squirts does it take to produce a gallon of milk from a cow?
a) 12
b) 120
c) 345
d) 450

331) True or false: Azaleas are poisonous to cats.

332> True or false: cats have 32 muscles in each ear.

★ ★

333) True or false: Dogs shouldn't eat grapes.

334) How long do Irish wolf hounds usually live?
   a) 6-8 years
   b) 8-10 years
   c) 10-12 years
   d) 12-15 years

335) True or false: There is a real disease called cat scratch fever.

★ ★

336) True or false: The fastest herbivore on Earth is the cheetah.

★ ★

337) True or false: Turkey eggs can have two yolks.

★ ★

338) True or false: Aardvark means "earthpig" in Afrikaans.

339) True or false: More than a million wildebeests have been known to herd in Tanzania and Kenya.

★ ★

340) TRUE OR FALSE: THERE IS NO MALE FOUR-HORNED ANIMAL.

★ ★

341) True or false: The American antelope can shed its horns every year.

★ ★

342) True or false: **The smallest camel species is the vicuna.**

343) Porcupines are
a) Nearsighted
b) Hard of hearing
c) Both
d) Neither

CHAPTER

6

344 > True or false: The Comics Code forbade showing unique methods of concealing weapons.

345) True or false: According to the Comics Code, kidnappers always had to be punished.

* *

346) True or false: The Comics Code stated that the word "horror" could be used in a comic book title.

* *

347) Did the Comics Code specifically restrict the ridicule of religion?

* *

348) True or false: The Comics Code stated that divorce could never be treated humorously.

349) True or false: The Comics Code stated that monkeys should never be presented as pets.

**350) Did the Comics Code
rule that tobacco couldn't be
advertised in comic books.**

* *

**351) Did the Comics Code rule that politicians
couldn't advertise in comic books.**

* *

**352) DID THE COMICS
CODE RULE THAT SEA
MONKEYS COULDN'T BE
SOLD IN COMIC BOOKS.**

* * * * * * * * * * *

**353) Did the Comics
Code rule that
fireworks couldn't be
sold in comic books?**

**354) Which came first:
DC or Marvel?**

**355) True or false: Marvel was
originally called Timely Comics.**

NAME THE COMIC BOOK HERO THAT MATCHES THE FOLLOWING SECRET IDENTITIES.

356 > Bruce Banner

• •

357 > Billy Batson

• •

358 > Betsy Braddock

• •

359 > Frank Castle

• •

360 > Linda Danvers

• •

361 > Barbara Gordon

• •

362 > Dick Grayson

• •

363 > Carter Hall

• •

364 > James "Logan" Howlett

365 > Clark Kent

366 > Peter Parker

367 > Diana Prince

368 > Kyle Rayner

369 > Steve Rogers

370 > Albert Simmons

371 > Tony Stark

372 > Bruce Wayne

373 > Wally West

374 > Eel O'Brian

375) Who showed up in comics first, Captain America or Captain Marvel?

376) In Tintin, what is Professor Calculus' physical challenge?
- a) A wooden leg
- b) He's hard of hearing
- c) He's blind in one eye
- d) He has three missing fingers

377) True or false: Until Steven Spielberg's film, Tintin has never been featured in a movie.

378) True or false: There are Tintin shops in Belgium and England.

379) In what year did Tintin first appear?
- a) 1912
- b) 1929
- c) 1938
- d) 1941

380) Did Tintin ever travel to the moon?

381) True or false: *Archie Comics #1* set a record for the highest price paid for a comic book.

382) TRUE OR FALSE: SABRINA THE TEENAGE WITCH IS A SPINOFF OF ARCHIE COMICS.

383) True or false: The American pop/rock group the Monkees was first conceived as recurring characters in Archie Comics.

384) True or false: Josie and the Pussycats is a spinoff of Archie Comics.

385) True of false: Archie has never appeared on a U.S. postage stamp.

* * * * * * * * * * * * * * * * * * *

386> How many brothers and sisters does Archie have?

* * * * * * * * * * * * * * * * * * *

387) True or false: The fictional band the Archies had an actual hit?

* *

388) What letter does Jughead usually have on his sweatshirt?

* * * * * * * * * * * * * * * * *

389) What is the name of the shop where the Archie crowd hangs out?
a) Pop Tate's Chok'lit Shoppe
b) Arnold's Drive In
c) Eat Here
d) The Peach Pit

* *

390) True or false: Josie was a character in Archie Comics for more than five years before she became leader of a band.

391) What was the innovation of the comic *Gasoline Alley?*
   a) Split panels
   b) Its characters aged
   c) No men were featured
   d) It had no words

****

392) Who is Blondie's husband?

****

393) Where did *The Far Side* first appear?
a) *The New York Times*
b) *The Philadelphia Inquirer*
c) *The Miami Herald*
d) *The San Francisco Chronicle*

****

394) WHICH LAUNCHED FIRST, *THE FAR SIDE* OR *BLOOM COUNTY?*

395) True or false: *Calvin and Hobbes* creator Bill Watterson didn't want any merchandise to be created based on his characters.

● ●

396) Who created *The Boondocks?*
a) Aaron McGruder
b) Maron McAuder
c) Garry McMurtry
d) Ali McAllister

397) Buck Rogers first appeared in the...
a) 1920s
b) 1930s
c) 1940s
d) 1950s

398 > What do most comic strips have that Prince Valiant doesn't?
a > Color
b > Multiple characters
c > Lines around the frames
d > Conversation and thought balloons

399) When was Garfield launched?
a) 1978   b) 1982   c) 1989   d) 1992

400) What is Garfield's favorite food?

401) What is the relationship between Linus and Lucy in Peanuts?

★ ★

402) Who is Snoopy's brother in Peanuts?

★ ★

403) Who is in love with Schroeder?

404) What does Marcy usually call Charlie Brown?

405) What color hair does the girl who Charlie Brown has a crush on have?

* *

406) DOES SNOOPY PLAY ON CHARLIE BROWN'S BASEBALL TEAM?

407) True or false: Snoopy didn't always walk only on his hind legs.

408) Did Charlie Brown's team ever win a baseball game?

* *

409) True or false: Lucy was the first person to pull a football away from Charlie Brown as he tried to kick it. * * * * * * * * * * * * * * *

* * * * * * * * * * * * * * * * *

410 > Which was the first *Peanuts* TV special?

411) True or false: Lucy once put Linus's blanket through a paper shredder and spread the pieces across the Atlantic Ocean.

412) What is Snoopy's nickname when he is wearing sunglasses?

413) Is Charlie Brown bald?

* *

414) Has Pig-Pen ever appeared clean?

415) Does Pig-Pen play an instrument in *A Charlie Brown Christmas?*

416) What position does Lucy usually play on the Peanuts baseball team?

* *

417) True or false: Snoopy has never been licensed for a Nintendo or Wii game.

418) WHAT DOES LINUS DO WITH BIRDS THAT ANNOY LUCY?

● ●

419) How much does Lucy traditionally charge for psychiatric help?

● ●

420) Did Lucy's pulling away of the football ever cost Charlie Brown's team a football game?

421) Lucy's dress is usually what color?

422> Do Charlie Brown and Peppermint Patty go to the same school?

423) Charles Schulz created more than_____
Peanuts strips.

a) 1,750
b) 17,500
c) 175,000
d) 50,000

CHAPTER

7

Celebrities

424) Soupy Sales: TV comedian or Campbell's cofounder?

★ ★

425) Don Shula: Legendary acting coach or football coach?

★ ★

426) Jodie Sweetin: *Full House* **actress or inventor of aspartame.**

★ ★

427) David Foster Wallace: Novelist or attempted presidential assassin?

428) Melvil Dewey: Muppeteer or developer of library organization system?

429) Harlan Fiske Stone: Fast-food pioneer or Supreme Court Chief Justice?

430) Frederick Austerlitz is better known as what famous dancer?

★ ★ ★ ★ ★ ★ ★ ★ ★ ★ ★ ★ ★

431) LESLIE L. KING JR. IS BETTER KNOWN AS WHAT FORMER U.S. PRESIDENT?

★ ★ ★ ★ ★ ★ ★ ★ ★ ★ ★ ★ ★

432) Allen Stuart Konigsberg is better known as what writer/actor/director?

★ ★ ★ ★ ★ ★ ★ ★ ★ ★ ★

433) True or false: Writer C.S. Lewis's given names were Clive Staples.

434) True or false: Leonard Slye is better known as Roy Rogers?

435> True or false: Harry S. Truman's middle name was Shippe.

436) Charles Q. Dawes: *Survivor* winner or U.S. vice president?

****

437) Eddie Rickenbacker: Racecar driver or German fighter pilot?

****

438) Johnnie Cochran: Lawyer or original cast member of *The Electric Company?*

****

439) Clive Barnes: Chef or theater critic?

****

440) Bella Abzug: American politician or German tycoon?

****

441) Bob Kane: Batman creator or fictional newspaper publisher?

****

442) Jeb Magruder: Civil War general or Watergate conspirator?

443) CHUCK CLOSE: FORMER ASTRONAUT OR PHOTO-REALIST PAINTER?

444) Jon Corzine: **U.S.** senator or Olympic bobsledder?

****

445) **Freeman Dyson: Physicist or infomercial pitchman?**

****

446) Ira Glass: Radio broadcaster or juggler?

****

447> Seymour Hersh: Investigative reporter or convicted embezzler?

448) Daniel Handler: Former New York City Mayor or children's book author?

449) Arianna Huffington: Website cofounder or cast member of Desperate Housewives?

450) Judith Jameson: Choreographer or fashion designer?

451) Richard Bachman: Pseudonym for Stephen King or chairman of Southwest Airlines?

452) Enrico Fermi: Scientist or chef?

453) Yuri Gagarin: Cosmonaut or Soviet politician?

454) Howard Hughes: Reclusive billionaire or magazine publisher?

455) SANDRA DAY O'CONNOR: SUFFRAGETTE OR SUPREME COURT JUSTICE?

456) Leni Riefenstahl: German filmmaker or founder of the American Kennel Club.

457) Are President Richard Nixon and actress Cynthia Nixon related?

458) Are author Ernest Hemingway and actress Mariel Hemingway related?

459> True or false: Novelist Nicholson Baker is actor Jack Nicholson's son.

460) Are actresses Rosalind Russell and Keri Russell related?

461) Are composers Johann and Richard Strauss related?

462) Are civil rights leader Jesse Jackson and baseball Hall of Famer Reggie Jackson related?

463) Are singer Dean and comedian Demetri Martin related?

PORTRAIT OF MOTHER

464) Are psychiatrist Sigmund Freud and artist Lucian Freud related?

465) Are artists Claude Monet and Eduard Manet related?

466) Are actress Anne Hathaway and the Anne Hathaway who married William Shakespeare related?

467) ARE ACTRESSES JULIA AND EMMA
ROBERTS RELATED?

468) Are actress Jane Seymour and Henry
VIII's wife Jane Seymour related?

469) Are basketball stars Reggie
and Cheryl Miller related?

470) Are singers Paul and Carly
Simon related?

471> Are actors Kirk and
Michael Douglas related?

472) What silent movie
star was known as the
Little Tramp?

473) What was William Cody's
nickname?

474) Who was known as the Butcher of Baghdad, Saddam Hussein or Fidel Castro?

★ ★

475) Henry Clay was known as The Great...
a) Henry C
b) Complainer
c) Compromiser
d) Consolidator

476) Garth Brooks is married to what fellow singer?
a) Patty Loveless
b) Kathy Mattea
c) Reba McEntire
d) Trisha Yearwood

477) Vince Gill is married to what fellow singer?
a) Amy Grant
b) Norah Jones
c) Sarah McLachlan
d) Linda Ronstadt

478) Elvis Costello is married to what fellow singer?

  a) Diana Krall
  b) Cleo Laine
  c) Patti Smith
  d) Dusty Springfield

479) BLAKE SHELTON IS MARRIED TO WHAT FELLOW SINGER?

  A) MIRANDA LAMBERT
  B) MARTINA MCBRIDE
  C) JENNIFER NETTLES
  D) CARRIE UNDERWOOD

480) Katy Perry was married to what comic actor?

  a) Russell Brand
  b) Jim Carrey
  c) Steve Coogan
  d) Ricky Gervais

CHAPTER

8

★★★★★★★★★

Music

481) What is the name of Eminem's alter ego?
   a) Slappy Sandy
   b) Slim Shady
   c) Slime Sally
   d) Slum Sammy

****

482) What legendary band was Robert Plant a part of?

****

483) How many members are there in the Black Keys?

****

What are the first names of...
   484) Crosby
   485) Stills
   486) Nash
   487) Young

****

488) How many Mamas and how many Papas were there in the Mamas and the Papas?

489) True or false: Gnarls Barkley consists of Cee Lo Green and Mighty Mouse.

490) TRUE OR FALSE: SINGER DRAKE PLAYED ONE OF THE TWO LEADS IN THE TV SERIES *DRAKE AND JOSH*.

* *

491) True or false: **Big Boi** was a member of OutKast.

* *

492) **Vampire Weekend is originally from...**
a) **Scotland**   b) **United States**
c) **Australia**   d) **England**

493) True or false: Arcade Fire got its name because its members worked in a Coney Island amusement arcade that burned down.

494 > Which of the following artists did Kanye West not produce for?

a > Alicia Keys   b > Ray Charles

c > Ludacris   d > Janet Jackson

● ● ● ● ● ● ● ● ● ● ● ● ● ● ● ● ● ● ●

495) MATCH THE MEMBER OF KISS TO HIS FACIAL MAKE-UP.

1) Gene Simmons
2) Paul Stanley
3) Ace Frehley
4) Peter Cris

a) Cat face
b) Stars around both eyes
c) Star around one eye
d) Wing-ish shapes around both eyes

● ● ● ● ● ● ● ● ● ● ● ● ● ● ● ● ● ● ●

496) What is the parenthetical addition to the title for the Doors' song "Break on Through"?

497) MATCH THE SONG TO THE BAND OR SINGER.

1) "Yellow Submarine"

2) "Do You Believe
in Magic?"

3) "Don't Worry Be Happy"

4) "Feeling Groovy"

5) "Daydream Believer"

a) The Lovin' Spoonful

b) The Beatles

c) Bobby McFerrin

d) The Monkees

e) Simon and
Garfunkel

498) What is the parenthetical addition to the title for the Billy Joel song "Movin' Out"?

• •

499) True or false: Wilco grew out of a band called Uncle Tupelo.

• •

500) True or false: The band called Breaks is known in the U.S. as Brakesbrakesbrakes.

• •

501) ARE THE AVETT BROTHERS (SCOTT, SETH, AND BOB) ACTUALLY ALL BROTHERS?

502) Which U2 album came first, *War* or *Achtung Baby?*

503) How many band members in U2?

504) Where does the band the Flaming Lips hail from?
   a) Oklahoma
   b) Florida
   c) Texas
   d) California

505> True or false: Tegan and Sara, of the band of the same name, are identical twins.

506) The Rolling Stones, the Beatles, the Doors or the Who: "She Loves You."

507) The Rolling Stones, the Beatles, the Doors or the Who: "Start Me Up."

508) The Rolling Stones, the Beatles, the Doors or the Who: "Substitute."

509) The president of Czechoslovakia named what American singer a special ambassador to the West?

a) Alice Cooper
b) Marilyn Manson
c) Bobby Vinton
d) Frank Zappa

510) What folk singer wrote "This Land Is Your Land"?

511) Which of the following is not a Beatles album?

a) *Revolver*
b) *Beatles for Sale*
c) *The Beatles '63*
d) *Rubber Soul*

512) Which of the following is not an album by Sheryl Crow?

a) *C'mon C'mon*
b) *100 Miles from Memphis*
c) *Detours*
d) *All This and More*

513) WHICH OF THE FOLLOWING IS NOT AN ALBUM BY JASON MRAZ?

A) MR. A-Z

B) TOPICS UNLIMITED

C) WE SING. WE DANCE. WE STEAL THINGS.

D) WAITING FOR MY ROCKET TO COME

514) Which of the following is not an album by Christina Aguilera?

a) *My Kind of Christmas*

b) *Mi Reflejo*

c) *Back to Basics*

d) *Running Away*

* *

515) Which of the following is not an album by Ben Folds?

a) *You Don't Know Me*

b) *Rockin' the Suburbs*

c) *Songs for Silverman*

d) *Way to Normal*

516) Which of the following is not an album by Cee Lo Green:

a) *Cee-Lo Green and His Perfect Imperfections*

b) *Cee-Lo Green Has It Down*

c) *Cee-Lo Green...Is the Soul Machine*

d) *The Lady Killer*

517 > Which of the following is not an album by Nelly Furtado:

    a > *Folklore*   b > *Whoa, Nelly!*

    c > *Loose*   d > *Nelly's Dream*

518) Which of the following is not an album by Beyonce Knowles:

a) *B'Day*   b) *I Am...Sasha Fierce*

c) *I Am...Yours*   d) *I Am...Tired*

* *

519) Which of the following is not an album by Kylie Minogue:

a) Intimate and Live   b) Pop It

c) Aphrodite   d) Body Language

520) What is the parenthetical addition to the title for the Offspring song "Pretty Fly"?

521) What is the parenthetical addition to the title for Rolling Stones song "Satisfaction"?

522) What is the parenthetical addition to the title for the R.E.M. song "It's the End of the World As We Know It "?

523) What is the parenthetical addition to the title for the Michael Jackson song "P.Y.T."?

524) What are the two parenthetical additions to the title for the Beastie Boys' song "Fight for Your Right"?

525) WHO WROTE THE SPANISH-ENGLISH CHRISTMAS HIT "FELIZ NAVIDAD"?
A) VIKKI CARR B) JOSE FELICIANO
C) JOSE GRECO   D) CARLOS SANTANA

526) Lil Wayne, Lil' Kim, or Lil Jon & The East Side Boyz: Who recorded "6 Foot 7 Foot"?

527) Was "Come to Me" a Puff Daddy, P. Diddy, or Diddy song?

528) Was "I Need a Girl (Part One)" a Puff Daddy, P. Diddy, or Diddy song?

529> Was "Bump, Bump, Bump" a Puff Daddy, P. Diddy, or Diddy song?

530) Was "Last Night" a Puff Daddy, P. Diddy, or Diddy song?

531) What singer wrote "The Christmas Song"?
   a) Tony Bennett
   b) Nat King Cole
   c) Dean Martin
   d) Mel Torme

532) What Rock and Roll Hall of Famer hit the Top 20 with "Rockin' Around the Christmas Tree" at age 16?

   a) Christina Aguilera
       b) Lesley Gore
        c) Brenda Lee
      d) Britney Spears

★ ★ ★ ★ ★ ★ ★ ★ ★ ★ ★

533) What Broadway composer, best known for *The Music Man*, wrote "It's Beginning to Look a Lot Like Christmas"?

a) Alan Jay Lerner   b) Richard Rodgers

c) Stephen Sondheim   d) Meredith Willson

534) Besides "The Chipmunk Song," what Christmas song by Alvin and the Chipmunks hit the Top 40?
a) Let It Snow! Let It Snow! Let It Snow!
b) Rudolph the Red-Nosed Reindeer
c) Santa Claus is Comin' to Town
d) Winter Wonderland

535) In "The Chipmunk Song," what present does Alvin really, really want?

★ ★ ★ ★ ★ ★ ★ ★ ★ ★ ★

536) True or false: The same composer wrote "Rudolph the Red-Nosed Reindeer" and "Rockin' Around the Christmas Tree."

537) WHAT BROADWAY COMPOSER WROTE "WHITE CHRISTMAS"?

    A) HAROLD ARLEN

    B) IRVING BERLIN

    C) JERRY HERMAN

    D) RICHARD RODGERS

538) What is the subtitle of John Lennon's "Happy Xmas"?

★ ★

539) Bob Dylan or the Beatles: *Blonde on Blonde?*

540) The Clash or Marvin Gaye: *London Calling?*

* *

541> The Rolling Stones or the Who: *Exile on Main Street?*

* *

542) The Monkees or the Beach Boys: *Pet Sounds?*

543) Miles Davis or Elvis Presley: *Kind of Blue?*

544) Jimi Hendrix or Janis Joplin: *Are You Experienced?*

* *

545) Bruce Hornsby or Bruce Springsteen: *Greetings from Asbury Park?*

* *

546) Nirvana or Coldplay: *Nevermind?*

547) Morrissey or Van Morrison: *Astral Weeks?*

● ● ● ● ● ● ● ● ● ● ● ● ● ● ● ● ● ● ● ●

548) Chuck Berry or Barry White: *The Great Twenty-Eight?*

● ● ● ● ● ● ● ● ● ● ● ● ● ● ● ● ● ● ● ●

549) MAC DAVIS OR FLEETWOOD MAC: *RUMORS?*

550) Iron & Wine or Coldplay: *A Rush of Blood to the Head?*

CHAPTER

9

★ ★ ★ ★ ★ ★ ★ ★ ★

It Happened In . . .

1994

551) What later presidential primary candidate became Speaker of the House in 1994?

a) Haven Hamilton
b) Newt Gingrich
c) Stephen Breyer
d) Aldrich Ames

552) Who won his first directing Oscar in 1994?

a) Chris Columbus
b) George Lucas
c) Steven Spielberg
d) Gerald R. Molen

553) What iconic 1969 peace, love, and music concert was reprised with a new list of performers including Green Day, Melissa Etheridge, and Metallica.

554) True or false: The White House launched its web page in 1994.

555) True or false: The New York Yankees beat the Houston Astros in the 1994 World Series.

556) NAFTA was established in 1994. What does it stand for?
- a) North American Federation of Teacher's Aides
- b) North American Free Trade Agreement
- c) Nebraska Anti-Federalist Trade Association
- d) No Arms for Turkey Association

557) Nancy Kerrigan's leg was clubbed in an attack in 1994. What sport did Kerrigan compete in?

558) What famous painting was stolen and then recovered in 1994?
- a) *The Mona Lisa*
- b) *Nude Descending a Staircase*
- c) *The Scream*
- d) *The Last Supper*

559) What did the Church of England do for the first time in 1994?
- a) Ordained female priests
- b) Allowed Irish to be clergy
- c) Paid taxes
- d) Established dioceses outside of the U.K.

560) It seems obvious, but what finally became Canada's official winter sport in 1994.

561) What did comet Shoemaker-Levy 9 collide with?
a) Mars   b) Jupiter   c) Earth   d) The Moon
****
562) It was announced in 1993 that former President Reagan had what disease?
✳✳✳✳✳✳✳✳✳✳✳✳✳✳✳✳✳✳✳✳✳✳✳✳
563) What future pop star, known for his music and his hair, was born in January of 1994?

1995

564) Which grossed more at the box office in 1995, *Die Hard with a Vengeance* or *Toy Story?*

565) Who is named President of France?
    a) Jacques LeClerc
    b) Jacques Damboise
    c) Jacques Chirac
    d) Jacques Indebox

566) What millionaire announced he would run for the Republican presidential nomination?

  a) Bill Gates   b) Steve Forbes
  c) Mark Zuckerberg   d) Donald Trump

567) The Million Man March was held in 1995 in Washington D.C. Who organized it?
a) Jon Stewart   b) Al Sharpton
c) Louis Farrakhan   d) James Watt

568) WHERE WAS YITZHAK RABIN ASSASSINATED?
  A) NEW YORK CITY   B) LONDON
  C) TEL AVIV   D) JERUSALEM

569) Rose Kennedy died in 1995. What was her relation to John F. Kennedy?

a) Mother   b) Sister   c) Wife   d) Daughter

* *

570) Butterfly McQueen died in 1995. What movie was the actress most famous for?

    a) *The Wizard of Oz*
    b) *Gone With the Wind*
    c) *Ben-Hur*
    d) *Apocalypse Now*

571) Where did the Rock and Roll Hall of Fame open in 1995?

• •

572> The Grammy for 1995 Song of the Year went to Bruce Springsteen's "Streets of Philadelphia." What movie was it from?

• • • • • • • • • • • • • • • • • • • ➤

573) Steve Fossett was the first person to do what solo?

        a) Ski down Mt. Everest
      b) Traverse the Sahara Desert
  c) Cross the Pacific Ocean in a balloon
     d) Compete on the Amazing Race

1996

574) What was the name of the computer that beat champion Garry Kasparov?
     a) Deep Red
     b) Deep Green
     c) Deep Purple
     d) Deep Blue

575) True or false: In 1996, Paula Abdul became the youngest person ever to win a Grammy for Album of the Year.

576) Who did Bill Clinton beat in the 1996 Presidential election?

577) What old school hotel in Las Vegas was imploded to clear space for the Venetian Hotel?
    a) The Palms
    b) The Sands
    c) Caesar's Palace
    d) The Trocadera

578) Jonathan Larson died just before the Broadway premiere of his musical. What was that show?

579) The star of *Singin' in the Rain* died in 1996. He was...
    a) Fred Astaire   b) Buddy Hackett
    c) Gene Kelly   d) Rudolph Valentino

580) WHO WAS NOMINATED TO BECOME THE FIRST FEMALE SECRETARY OF STATE IN 1996?

 A) RUTH BADER GINSBURG
 B) MADELEINE ALBRIGHT
 C) HILLARY CLINTON
 D) RUTH BUZZI

...AND IT HASN'T INCREASED SINCE THEN!

581) True or false: **The median household income in the U.S in 1996 was less than $40,000?**

* * * * * * * * *

582) **What gangsta rapper was found shot and later died in 1996?**

a) **Ice-T**
b) **Ice Cube**
c) **Tupac Shakur**
d) **Talia Shire**

583) Frank McCourt's bestselling book *Angela's Ashes* concerned growing up poor in what country?

 a) Israel
 b) Egypt
 c) Ireland
 d) Poland

584 > Who won the 1996 Emmy for Best Actor in a Comedy Series for his role in *3rd Rock from the Sun?*

a > John Lithgow b > Rip Torn

c > Tim Conway d > Dennis Miller

★ ★ ★ ★ ★ ★ ★ ★ ★ ★ ★ ★ ★ ★ ★ ★ ★ ★ ★

585) In 1996, what percentage of American homes had a computer?

a) 33% b) 44% c) 55% d) 66%

1997

586) Who became Prime Minster of England in 1997?

a) Tony Scott b) Tony Undershaft

c) Tony Blair d) Tony Thatcher

★ ★ ★ ★ ★ ★ ★ ★ ★ ★ ★ ★ ★ ★ ★ ★ ★ ★ ★

587) In June of 1997, dictator Pol Pot fled from his stronghold in what country?

a) Laos b) Cambodia

c) Senegal d) Nigeria

588) What venerable department store folded in 1997?

a) F.W. Woolworth b) P.J. O'Hullygully

c) G.W. Murphey d) P.T. Barnum

589) More than two million people around the world watched whose funeral in 1997?

* *

590) WHAT COUNTRY OPTED TO LAUNCH ITS OWN PARLIAMENT IN 1997?

    A) SPAIN   B) AUSTRALIA

    C) SCOTLAND   D) IRAN

* *

591) What movie, released in December 1997, became the highest-grossing movie in history—at least, until *Avatar* came along?

* *

592) True or false: The first hybrid car to go into full production was the Toyota Prius.

* *

593) Allen Ginsberg, who died in 1997, was famous for being a...

    a) Speed skater   b) Mountaineer

    c) Poet   d) Cartoonist

* *

594 > True or false: In *The Terminator,* made in 1984, the nuclear war took place in 1997.

* *

595) The TV rating system debuted in 1997. What rating is between TV-PG and TV-M?

596) Prince Michael Junior is born. Who is his famous father?

1998

597) The Unibomber pleaded guilty in 1998. Did he get a life sentence or the death penalty?

598) Which grossed more at the box office, *Armageddon* or *A Bug's Life*?

599) Which won the Oscar for Best Film, *Saving Private Ryan* or *Shakespeare in Love*?

600) Britney Spears released her debut single in 1998. What song was it?

601) Who staged more nuclear tests in 1998, India or Pakistan?

602) WHO WON THE STANLEY CUP, DETROIT OR WASHINGTON?

603) What television sitcom, starring a famous comedian, aired its last episode in 1998 with about 76 million viewers watching?

604) One of the world's most famous singers died in 1998 at the age of 82. Who was he?

605) Where did the Athena probe find frozen water?

    a) Mars
    b) Venus
    c) Mercury
    d) The Moon

606> Who won the Olympic figure skating gold medal in 1998?

    a> Tara Lipinksi   b> Holly Alexander

    c> Oksana Baiul   d> Nicole Bobek

607) Who broke Roger Maris's single-season home run record by hitting 70 in 1998?

608) True or false: President Bill Clinton was impeached.

1999

609) What is the name of the European currency that was established in 1999?

• •

610) Who became President of Venezuela in 1999?
- a) Hugo Boss
- b) Hugo Chavez
- c) Hugo Victor
- d) Hugo Castro

• •

611) What music sharing service had its debut—and caused controversy in the music business?

• •

612) Brandi Chastain scored the game-winning point in a big game against China in what sport?
- a) Volleyball
- b) Soccer
- c) Softball
- d) Basketball

• •

613) Who won the Tour de France in 1999?

• •

614) WHAT TWO COMPANIES, PRIMARILY KNOWN FOR GASOLINE, MERGED IN 1999?

A) EXXON AND SHELL   B) MOBIL AND SHELL

C) SHELL AND CONESTO   D) EXXON AND MOBIL

615) Who resigned as President of Russia?
   a) Boris Yeltsin
   b) Vladimir Putin
   c) Mikhail Gorbachev
   d) Vladislav Surkov

616) The son of what former president died in a plane crash.

617) Who sang a 1982 song encouraging listeners to "party like it's 1999"?

618) What is the name of the virus that raised concerns about possible massive computer breakdowns at the end of the year.

619) Universal Music Group was formed in 1999 from the merger of what two record labels?
   a) Universal and Polygram   b) Warner Bros. and Apple
   c) K-TI and Virgin   d) Polymer and Polygram

620) What actor left the hit show ER for what would become a very successful movie career?

621) What low-budget horror film went on to become the most profitable film of all time?

622) What went over 150 million in 1999?

a) The number of cell-phone owners

b) The number of people in China

c) The number of Internet users around the world

d) The number of dogs in America

2000

623) In Florida, 6-year-old Elian Gonzalez made headlines after he was forced to return to his native country. What country?

a) El Salvador b) Peru

c) Cuba d) Russia

624) A close presidential election in the U.S. brought attention to the voting cards used. What term was used to describe situations where votes weren't clear?

a) Muddy vote b) Hanging chad

c) Vague vote d) Partial confusion

625) WHO WAS AL GORE'S RUNNING MATE IN THE 2000 ELECTION?

    A) WALTER MONDALE B) BOB DOLE

    C) JOE LIEBERMAN   D) JOHN KERRY

* * * * * * * * * * * * *

626) Charles Schulz died in 2000. What is he best known for creating?

* * * * * * * * * * * * *

627) Who opted to leave the morning show program she co-hosted with Regis Philbin?

628) What is the name of the magazine the Oprah Winfrey launched in 2000?

629> Was 2000 a leap year?

* *

630) Where were the 2000 Summer Olympics held?

    a) China   b) Australia

    c) Finland d) South Africa

631) Who became the first former first lady of the U.S. to be elected to a public office when she became a senator for New York?

632) What won the Emmy Award for Outstanding Drama Series: *The West Wing* or *The Sopranos?*

****

633) True or false: In 2000, American Online purchased Universal Studios.

****

634) Who won the St. Louis vs. Tennessee Super Bowl?

****

635) Who won the Indiana vs. Los Angeles NBA Championship?

2001

636) What number president did George W. Bush become when he took office in January of 2001?

637) WHAT FELL INTO THE PACIFIC OCEAN IN MARCH OF 2001?

A) AN ASTEROID
B) THE RUSSIAN SPACE STATION MIR
C) VICE PRESIDENT DICK CHENEY
D) A PLANE FULL OF WILD TURKEYS

638) Junichiro Koizumi became prime minster of what country?

a) Japan b) Indonesia
c) Vietnam d) Cambodia

639) What is the flight number of the plane that is brought down in Shanksville, PA, during the World Trade Center/Pentagon attacks?

a) Flight 90 b) Flight 91
c) Flight 92 d) Flight 93

640) In what month did the U.S. invade Afghanistan in response to the 9/11 attacks?

a) September b) October
c) November d) December

641> What big Houston-based company filed for bankruptcy in December 2001?

a> Exxon   b> Enderon   c> Enron   d> Eldon

642) In what year were both the movie and the novel *2001: A Space Odyssey* by Arthur C. Clarke, released?

a) 1960   b) 1968   c) 1972   d) 1978

643) What band performed the 2001 Grammy-winning Record of the Year "Beautiful Day"?

644) What long-running film series was launched on November 4, 2011?

a) *Star Wars*   b) *Lord of the Rings*

c) *The Fast and the Furious*   d) *Harry Potter*

645) Isaac Stern died in 2001. What was he famous for playing?

a) Baseball   b) The piano   c) The violin   d) Basketball

646) What powdered substance caused a scare when found in the U.S. mail?

a) Cocaine   b) Anthrax

c) Regolith   d) Titanium

647) How many days did Pennsylvania miners spend trapped in a mine?

a) 44
b) 55
c) 66
d) 77

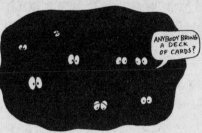

ANYBODY BRING A DECK OF CARDS?

648) Who won in the New England vs. St. Louis Super Bowl?

649) Who won at Wimbledon when Venus Williams competed against her sister Serena Williams?

650) Who won the World Cup, Brazil or Germany?

651) True or false: The Osbournes won an Emmy for Best Reality Series.

652) TRUE OR FALSE: DENZEL WASHINGTON WAS THE FIRST AFRICAN-AMERICAN TO WIN THE OSCAR FOR BEST ACTOR.

653) What superhero was the subject of 2002's top box-office grossing film?

654) What New York mayor was given an honorary knighthood by the Queen of England?
a) **Rudy Giuliani**   b) **Ed Koch**
c) **Michael Bloomberg**   d) **David Dinkins**

655) Dave Thomas died in 2002. What fast food franchise did he create?

656 > A woman burning a letter from her husband led to a wildfire that destroyed more than 130 houses in what state?

a > West Virginia   b > Colorado
c > Pennsylvania   d > California

657) What country club, home of the Masters Tournament, came under fire for not admitting women as members?
a) Atlanta Springs   b) Georgia Pines
c) Augusta National   d) Oak Valley

658) Where were the 2002 Winter Olympics held?

a) Salt Lake City   b) Los Angeles
c) Chicago   d) Atlanta

2003

659) What country joined the U.S. in launching a war against Iraq?

****

660) In 2003, Palestine announced its first what?

a) Nuclear treaty   b) McDonald's
c) Prime minister   d) Symphony orchestra

****

661) What space shuttle exploded as it reentered Earth's atmosphere?

****

662) True or false: Arnold Schwarzenegger was the first actor to become governor of California.

****

663) WHO WON A GRAMMY AWARD FOR "DON'T KNOW WHY"?

****

664) True or false: *Chicago* became the first musical ever to win an Academy Award for Best Picture.

665) Strom Thurmond died in 2003. He was a/an _____.
a) Politician   b) Athlete
c) Wall Street trader   d) Restaurateur

••••••••••••••••••••••••••••••••••••••

666) The supersonic jet the Concorde flew its last commercial flight in 2003. When was its first commercial flight?

 a) 1964   b) 1969   c) 1976   d) 1982

****

667 > What angry-sounding disease effected cattle in Washington State?

••••••••••➤

668) True or false: An earthquake struck the Iranian city of Bam.

****

669) About 50 million Americans and Canadians lost power for two days because of power line failures in what state?
     a) New York   b) Texas
     c) California   d) Ohio

670) Why did *New York Times* reporter Jason Blair resign?
a) Conflict of interest because of his website
b) He bought the paper
c) Plagiarism
d) None of the above

2004

671) True or false: The United Nations declared 2004 the International Year of Rice.

672) After 17 years, the U.S. lifted a ban on travel to what country?
- a) North Korea
- b) Cuba
- c) Libya
- d) El Salvador

673) Who won the Formula One World Drivers Championship for the 7th time?
a) Mario Andretti
b) Michael Schumacher
c) Al Unser, Jr.
d) Takai Katai

674) The Boston Red Sox won the World Series in 2004. When was the last time they had won?
a) 1965   b) 1954   c) 1932   d) 1918

675) WHO RESIGNED AS U.S. SECRETARY OF STATE IN 2004?

A) CONDOLEEZZA RICE   B) COLIN POWELL
C) HILLARY CLINTON   D) GUS GIVERSON

676) The world's tallest bridge opens. Where is it located?
a) France b) Italy c) Spain d) Germany

677) What controversial religious film was a blockbuster hit for director Mel Gibson?

678) Because of the lockout, there was no Stanley Cup in hockey for the first time since what year?
a) 1919 b) 1925 c) 1945 d) 1950

679 > What band had a 2004 hit with "Accidentally in Love"?

2005

680) A 20-year civil war ended in what country?
a) Ethiopia b) Sudan c) Peru d) Indonesia

681) After Pope John Paul died, Pope Benedict took over. What Roman number follows Benedict's name?

a) X   b) V   c) XV   d) XVI

682) What was the name of the hurricane that caused considerable damage to the Gulf Coast?

683) Who became the 17th Chief Justice of the Supreme Court?

a) John Jay   b) Robert James

c) John Roberts   d) Robert Johnson

684) The 2005 Record of the Year "Here We Go Again" was a collaboration between Norah Jones and...

a) Tony Bennett
b) Ray Charles
c) Stevie Wonder
d) Steve Lawrence

685) What replaced heart disease as the top cause of death for people under the age of 85?

686) French surgeons performed the first human _ _ _ _ _ transplant.
a) Foot
b) Brain
c) Face
d) Double lung

NEXT TIME, WE HOPE TO USE A HUMAN FACE!

687) IN 2005, WHICH HAD A LARGER POPULATION, EUROPE OR AFRICA?

2006

688) Who declared that Pluto was not a planet?
a) The International Astronomical Society
b) The Committee for Astronomical Investigation
c) NASA
d) The International Planetary Society

689) What was the price of the record-setting sale of Jackson Pollock's *No. 5, 1948?*

    a) $8 million   b) $18 million

    c) $80 million   d) $140 million

690) What were the jobs of the main characters in the Christopher Nolan movie *The Prestige,* starring Hugh Jackman and Christian Bale?

* *

691 > Whose solo album *B'Day* went to number one on the Billboard charts?

* *

692) Who did Pittsburgh defeat in Super Bowl XL?

* *

693) Who did St. Louis defeat in the 2006 World Series?

* *

694) *Jersey Boys* won the Tony Award for Best Musical. What singing group is the musical about?

a) The Four Tops   b) The Four Freshmen

c) The Four Lads   d) The Four Seasons

695) Where were the 2006 Winter Olympics held?
a) Austria   b) United States   c) Italy   d) Finland

2007

696) In 2007, archeologists in Japan found a 2,100-year-old what?
a) Apple
b) Melon
c) Orange
d) Banana

****

697) What book, released in 2007, became the fastest selling book ever?

****

698) What group of Hollywood professionals went on strike in 2007?
a) Cinematographers   b) Actors
c) Writers   d) Editors

699) WHAT FORMER VICE PRESIDENT OF THE UNITED STATES WON A NOBEL PEACE PRIZE IN 2007?
A) WALTER MONDALE   B) DAN QUAYLE
C) ALBERT GORE JR.   D) SPIRO AGNEW

700) Nicolas Sarkozy beat Segolene Royal in what country's presidential elections?

701) Who became the first woman speaker of the house in the U.S. in 2007?

★ ★

702) How much did the U.S. minimum wage go up to in 2007?

a) $4.45   b) $5.15   c) $5.85   d) $6.76

★ ★

703 > Who did Indianapolis beat in Super Bowl XLI?

2008

704) What country held its first general election in 2008?

a) Congo   b) Philippines   c) Mexico   d) Bhutan

★ ★

705) How many satellites did India send into orbit on one launch, setting a world record?

a) 5   b) 7   c) 10   d) 12

★ ★

706) How many gold medals did Michael Phelps win at the 2008 Summer Olympics?

707) Who was Barack Obama's vice presidential running mate in 2008?

★ ★

708) True or false: A leap second was added at the end of 2008.

709) Charlton Heston died in 2008. Which of the following was not one of his movies:

  a) *The Ten Commandments*
  b) *Planet of the Apes*
  c) *The Great Escape*
  d) *The Omega Man*

710) Which 2008 release grossed more at the box office, *Kung Fu Panda* or *Madagascar: Escape 2 Africa?*

★ ★

711) WHAT *SATURDAY NIGHT LIVE* CAST MEMBER FAMOUSLY IMPERSONATED VICE PRESIDENTIAL CANDIDATE SARAH PALIN?

ANSWERS

★★★★★★★★

1) *Ben-Hur*
2) *Titanic*
3) *The Lord of the Rings: The Return of the King*
4) a
5) *Avatar*
6) false
7) true
8) true
9) *Success*
10) *Cuckoo's*
11) *Runner*
12) *Paris*
13) *Louis*
14) *Snatches*
15) *Queen*
16) *Mockingbird*
17) *Northwest*
18) *Mohicans*
19) true
20) true
21) *Boys*
22) *Independence*
23) *West*
24) *State*
25) *Black*
26) *Tale*
27) *Pursuit*
28) *Legend*
29) *Pounds*
30) "Yes we can"
31) c
32) Read
33) Dora
34) b
35) true
36) b
37) d
38) *Touched by an Angel* (212)
39) *Everybody Loves Raymond* (210)
40) true
41) true
42) false
43) false
44) The Learning Channel
45) Black Entertainment Television
46) false
47) Headline News
48) true
49) c
50) Home Shopping Network
51) Quality, Value, Convenience
52) true
53) true
54) true
55) false
56) true
57) true
58) true
59) d
60) c
61) b
62) c
63) b
64) c
65) a
66) d

67) d
68) b
69) b
70) a
71) d
72) c
73) true
74) b
75) Sparky Anderson
76) true
77) Cito Gaston
78) c
79) d
80) a
81) a
82) b
83) d
84) c
85) a
86) b
87) d
88) a
89) b
90) c
91) c
92) Central
93) Pacific
94) Northwest
95) Southwest
96) Southeast
97) less
98) red, white, and blue
99) double dribble
100) b
101) c

102) true
103) Wilt Chamberlain
104) Michael Jordan
105) Elgin Baylor
106) Jerry West
107) Michael Jordan
108) Moses Malone
109) Moses Malone
110) UCLA
111) Brazil
112) true
113) yes
114) yes
115) Germany
116) true
117) a
118) a
119) Finland
120) Canada
121) false
122) b
123) true
124) Dave Andreychuk
125) fifteen
126) c
127) b
128) false—it's considered "illegal pinfall"
129) false—fiber is that part we can't digest
130) true
131) d
132) coconut
133) dates
134) true

135) sauce
136) false—it means "in chili."
137) true
138) no—it comes from Europe
139) all together
140) with meat
141) a
142) true
143) true
144) Frosted Flakes
145) uncooked
146) Champions
147) Kix
148) c
149) b
150) false—Sugar Pops
151) true
152) true
153) 1 d, 2 a, 3 b, 4 e, 5 c
154) d
155) one
156) False—five grams or more
157) off the tree
158) Mikey
159) Trix
160) Total
161) Horatio
162) Mayor McCheese
163) a
164) Yo quiero Taco Bell
165) Sonic
166) b
167) false—they are also in some movie theaters
168) Roy Rogers
169) Big Mac
170) square
171) b
172) b
173) cows
174) true
175) false
176) true
177) true
178) true
179) c
180) true
181) true
182) *Forest Gump*
183) false
184) no
185) medicine
186) darker
187) France
188) brown
189) true
190) true
191) b
192) true
193) Oreo
194) plain
195) d
196) d
197) b
198) c
199) a
200) d

201) b
202) d
203) Chocolate Swamp
204) true
205) c
206) four
207) ten
208) one
209) colonel
210) lieutenant
211) forty
212) sixty-three
213) you move and then roll again
214) thirteen
215) true
216) four
217) royal flush
218) scissors
219) two
220) red
221) two
222) yellow
223) c
224) five
225) two
226) true
227) false
228) true
229) true
230) false—it has a spinning apple
231) c
232) c
233) nine

234) Chaotic-Evil
235) d
236) magic missiles
237) b
238) false—*The Dragon*
239) b
240) no
241) true
242) fifteen spaces
243) yes
244) one
245) a
246) false
247) true
248) yes
249) yes
250) no
251) no
252) true
253) b
254) ten
255) true
256) c
257) false
258) false
259) Mediterranean and Baltic
260) Reading, B&O, Short Line, Pennsylvania
261) Community Chest
262) true
263) forty
264) twenty-eight
265) true
266) false—1960s

267) eighty-one
268) nine
269) six
270) true
271) false
272) d
273) yes
274) true
275) true
276) four
277) false
278) true
279) false
280) true
281) females
282) b
283) male
284) ridged
285) yes
286) false—they are for killing
287) dot
288) cheetah
289) male
290) five
291) true
292) yes
293) five
294) b
295) tiger
296) c
297) body
298) a
299) false—omnivores
300) false

301) true
302) c
303) ring-tailed coati
304) always dark
305) false—it's the moose
306) c
307) true
308) true
309) Indian
310) Sumatran
311) white rhino
312) false
313) three
314) false—they eat that every day
315) marsupial
316) false
317) false
318) Australia
319) d
320) true
321) false—they have soft footpads to better walk quietly in the jungle
322) true
323) five
324) true
325) false—five inches is about the maximum
326) gray
327) lower
328) a bilby
329) a
330) c

331) true
332) true
333) true
334) a
335) true
336) false—the North American pronghorn is faster
337) true
338) true
339) true
340) false—the male four-horned antelope has a quartet of them
341) true
342) true
343) a
344) true
345) true
346) false
347) yes
348) false
349) false
350) yes
351) no
352) no
353) yes
354) DC
355) true
356) The Incredible Hulk
357) Captain Marvel
358) Psylocke
359) The Punisher
360) Supergirl
361) Batgirl
362) Robin
363) Hawkman
364) Wolverine
365) Superman
366) Spider-Man
367) Wonder Woman
368) Green Lantern
369) Captain America
370) Spawn
371) Iron Man
372) Batman
373) The Flash
374) Plastic-Man
375) Captain Marvel
376) b
377) false
378) true
379) b
380) yes
381) false—but it did set the record for highest price for a non-superhero comic book
382) true
383) false
384) true
385) false
386) none
387) true—"Sugar, Sugar"
388) S
389) a
390) true
391) b
392) Dagwood
393) d

394) *The Far Side*—but both were in 1980
395) true
396) a
397) a
398) d
399) a
400) Lasagna
401) brother and sister
402) Spike
403) Lucy
404) Charles
405) red
406) yes
407) true
408) yes
409) false—Violet did it first, in a 1951 comic strip
410) *A Charlie Brown Christmas*
411) false
412) Joe Cool
413) no, not completely
414) yes
415) yes—the double bass
416) right field (sometimes center field)
417) false
418) pats them on the head
419) five cents
420) yes
421) blue
422) no
423) b
424) TV comedian
425) football coach
426) *Full House* actress
427) novelist
428) developer of library organization system
429) Supreme Court Chief Justice
430) Fred Astaire
431) Gerald Ford
432) Woody Allen
433) true
434) true
435) false—it stood for itself
436) U.S. vice president
437) racecar driver
438) lawyer
439) theater critic
440) American politician
441) Batman creator
442) Watergate conspirator
443) photo-realist painter
444) U.S. senator
445) physicist
446) radio broadcaster
447) investigative reporter
448) children's book author
449) website cofounder
450) choreographer
451) pseudonym for Stephen King
452) scientist
453) cosmonaut
454) reclusive billionaire

455) Supreme Court justice
456) German filmmaker
457) no
458) yes
459) false
460) no
461) no
462) no
463) no
464) yes
465) no
466) no
467) yes
468) no
469) yes
470) no
471) yes
472) Charlie Chaplin
473) Buffalo Bill
474) Saddam Hussein
475) c
476) d
477) a
478) a
479) a
480) a
481) b
482) Led Zeppelin
483) two
484) David
485) Stephen
486) Graham
487) Neil
488) two each

489) false—Cee Lo Green and Danger Mouse
490) false
491) true
492) b
493) false
494) b
495) 1 d, 2 c, 3 b, 4 a
496) 1 b, 2 a, 3 c, 4 e, 5 d
497) (To the Other Side)
498) (Anthony's Song)
499) true
500) true
501) no—but Scott and Seth are
502) *War*
503) four
504) a
505) true
506) The Beatles
507) Rolling Stones
508) The Who
509) d
510) Woody Guthrie
511) c
512) d
513) b
514) d
515) a
516) b
517) d
518) d
519) b
520) (For a White Guy)
521) (I Can't Get No)

522) (And I Feel Fine)
523) (Pretty Young Thing)
524) (You Gotta), (to Party!)
525) b
526) Lil Wayne
527) Diddy
528) P. Diddy
529) P. Diddy
530) Diddy
531) d
532) c
533) d
534) b
535) a hula hoop
536) true
537) b
538) War Is Over
539) Bob Dylan
540) The Clash
541) The Rolling Stones
542) The Beach Boys
543) Miles Davis
544) Jimi Hendrix
545) Bruce Springsteen
546) Nirvana
547) Van Morrison
548) Chuck Berry
549) Fleetwood Mac
550) Coldplay
551) b
552) c
553) Woodstock
554) true

555) false—There was no World Series in 1994
556) b
557) figure skating
558) c
559) a
560) hockey
561) b
562) Alzheimer's
563) Justin Bieber
564) *Die Hard with a Vengeance*
565) c
566) b
567) c
568) c
569) a
570) b
571) Cleveland
572) *Philadelphia*
573) c
574) d
575) false—but Alanis Morissette did
576) Bob Dole
577) b
578) *Rent*
579) c
580) b
581) true
582) c
583) c
584) a
585) b
586) c

587) b
588) a
589) Diana, Princess of Wales
590) c
591) *Titanic*
592) true
593) c
594) true
595) TV-14
596) Michael Jackson
597) life sentence
598) *Armageddon*
599) *Shakespeare in Love*
600) "...Baby One More Time"
601) Pakistan
602) Detroit
603) *Seinfeld*
604) Frank Sinatra
605) d
606) a
607) Mark McGwire
608) yes—but did not have to leave office
609) the Euro
610) b
611) Napster
612) b
613) Lance Armstrong
614) d
615) a
616) John F. Kennedy
617) Prince
618) Y2K
619) a

620) George Clooney
621) *The Blair Witch Project*—although that honor now belongs to the 2009 movie *Paranormal Activity*
622) c
623) c
624) b
625) c
626) the *Peanuts* comic strip and characters
627) Kathy Lee Gifford
628) O
629) yes
630) b
631) Hillary Clinton
632) *The West Wing*
633) false—it purchased Time Warner
634) St. Louis
635) Los Angeles
636) 43
637) b
638) a
639) d
640) b
641) c
642) b
643) U2
644) d
645) c
646) b
647) d
648) New England

649) Serena Williams
650) Brazil
651) true
652) false
653) Spider-man
654) a
655) Wendy's
656) b
657) c
658) a
659) England
660) c
661) Columbia
662) false—Ronald Reagan
was also an actor
663) Norah Jones
664) false
665) a
666) c
667) mad cow disease
668) true
669) d
670) c
671) true
672) c
673) b
674) d
675) b
676) a
677) *The Passion of the
Christ*
678) a
679) Counting Crows
680) b
681) d
682) Katrina

683) c
684) b
685) cancer
686) c
687) Africa
688) a
689) d
690) magicians
691) Beyonce
692) Seattle
693) Detroit
694) d
695) c
696) b
697) *Harry Potter and the
Deathly Hallows*
698) c
699) c
700) France
701) Nancy Pelosi
702) c
703) Chicago
704) d
705) c
706) eight
707) Joe Biden
708) true
709) c
710) *Kung Fu Panda*
711) Tina Fey

About Applesauce Press

GOOD IDEAS RIPEN WITH TIME. FROM SEED TO HARVEST,
APPLESAUCE PRESS CREATES BOOKS WITH BEAUTIFUL
DESIGNS, CREATIVE FORMATS, AND KID-FRIENDLY INFORMATION.
LIKE OUR PARENT COMPANY, CIDER MILL PRESS
BOOK PUBLISHERS, OUR PRESS BEARS FRUIT TWICE A YEAR,
PUBLISHING A NEW CROP OF TITLES EACH SPRING AND FALL.

"WHERE GOOD BOOKS ARE READY FOR PRESS"
VISIT US ON THE WEB AT
WWW.CIDERMILLPRESS.COM
OR WRITE TO US AT
12 PORT FARM ROAD
KENNEBUNKPORT, MAINE 04046